How to Write a Book in Ten Minutes a Day

Denice Simms

Stay in touch with the author by subscribing. To subscribe, visit www. Denicesimms.com for details.

ISBN 978-1-989427-57-6
ISBN 978-1-989427-58-3

Copyright © 2021 Denice Simms. All rights reserved.

Table of Contents

Page 3 - Introduction
Page 6 - Formatting
Page 10 - Creating a Reference Document
Page 16 - Hooking
Page 20 - Writing Techniques
Page 31 - Start Writing Your Next Book
Page 34 - 10 Common Mistakes Made in Your First Draft
Page 41 - Writer's Block/Stuck Writing a Scene?
Page 42 – Five Key Elements to Writing a Gripping Story
Page 44 – The First Paragraph
Page 50 - Luck is What You Have Left After You Give 100%
Page 53 – How to Format Your Book in Ten Minutes a Day
Page 55 - Keep in Touch
Page 56 - Did You Enjoy This Book?
Page 57 - Author's Note

Introduction

Hey there! Welcome! In case you're wondering, this is not my first published book. This is a pen name I'm using to segregate another brand and genre from my other works. My writing career began back in 2010 under the pen name Sandy Appleyard, and I added another pen name to my repertoire in 2019, Sandra Alex. If you'd like to check out any of my work, I offer the first books in all my series for free, so you're welcome to go see what I write, and what I'm talking about as I pen this book.

I write mostly romance, but I have written some romantic suspense, police procedurals, young adult suspense, and a couple of memoirs. Most of what I write is in series, however, I do have some standalones in my backlist, too. So, as you can tell, I have a lot of experience in the field. Also, just about everything I've done has been done by me, with few exceptions. Writing, editing, formatting, website design, some cover designing, ad copy, marketing, advertising, I've done it all myself, so I do know a thing or two about the literary world.

The book, and the series of books that will follow this one, came from my desire to share all the knowledge that I've garnered since I started writing. I've been asked many times, 'how do you do this?', and I'd love to be able to say, 'hey, pick up this book, it'll show you how to do just that, step by step', because frankly, if I had a dime for every time I've been asked how I do my writing stuff....

The Basics

When I first started out, I had a copy of Word from Microsoft Office, a hard drive, a USB memory stick, and that's it. For the most part, it was good, and worked well, but for those few instances where I had a corrupt memory stick, or my hard drive crashed, or worse, I was on the road and everything crashed, it was heartbreaking to say the least. While I don't use Scrivener or any fancy software, I do recommend purchasing a Microsoft Office package subscription, because in doing so, you also get cloud storage (via OneDrive), and mobile access with an app (that you can download from the app store for free). These two features have been life saving for me as a writer, because as long as I have a wifi source (I have data on my phone if I'm in a pinch), I can work, save and do anything I need to do with my work, anywhere.

The mobile Word app is especially handy because I can literally write anywhere. It's not great for formatting, but if I'm not by a laptop and I have a few minutes to spare, I write on my phone. It's easy and it automatically saves your work (although I do recommend exiting out of the app entirely when you're about to leave a wifi area, or you may lose the work you just finished. Logging out prompts an autosave, so you won't lose what you worked on the last time you saved), and it's a godsend. I've written so much while waiting in lines or doing something mundane that requires little or no focus, and it's a huge time saver.

For the Working Writer

This book is for the working writer, who has limited time to write a book. Limited time, meaning, small amounts of time each day, but with a somewhat unlimited time frame (approximately eight months to twelve months, depending on how many words you want your book to be). This is <u>not</u> a book with a 'get rich quick by writing a book instantly' scheme. If that's what you're looking for, you will not find it here. If you are a person who has written a book or who wants to write a book, and have limited daily time for which to accomplish it in, this book will help guide you with proven tips on how to do that.

In my writing career, I have written over thirty novels, doing so while working a full-time job with two children, a husband, and a house to keep up. If I can do it, you can do it, but only if you put your mind to it, and if you adopt the steps that I explain to you in this book.

Quick and Concise

There are <u>over twenty-five tips</u>. I'll give you **tips on every page**, starting from <u>page one</u> (as you see above, I've already provided you with a few tips!). Tips that you can start doing right now. If you have as little as ten minutes each day to write, I can show you how to complete an entire manuscript.

Self-discipline is key here, so if you're a person who has the ability to set your mind to doing something, you can accomplish this task.

In this book you'll find simple tips on how to write a book with little time in the first section, and I provide editing and other tips that I found helpful when I first started writing. Everything from writer's block to formatting to editing your manuscript.

Since 2010 I've been self-publishing my work, and during the time that I am writing this work I have over thirty works to my credit, using three pen names.

<u>Let's get started.</u>

Formatting

Many of the simplest things I learned about writing and launching a book were garnered from making **mistakes**. Lots of mistakes. And the first thing I'll tell you before you even open up a new Word document (assuming you're using Word) to start your book, is to **set your formatting first**. Unless you want to write an entire manuscript, edit it, and then learn that you have to turn around and format it from chapter one, I suggest you pay attention.

Chapter Headings

Many authors use the 'Heading 1' style when adding in their chapter headings, but I suggest you do not use this method. If you're not going to use a table of contents, it's okay, but if you are, do not use the heading paragraph style, as it confuses Word (if you're using Word), and your table of contents will not work properly, and it'll cause errors when uploading. I simply use a larger font size and center the heading.

Most of my books, at least the more recent ones, including this one, I use the font style 'Bookman Old Style', in size 12 for the text, and in size 16 for the chapter headings. It's a desirable font, easy to read, and is clear and concise when reading. Times New Roman is too heavy and harder on the eyes, so I would steer clear of that, which most Word documents default to, and Calibri, another commonly used font, is too small and lumped together. You can try whatever font you want, and it's easy to change it, but I prefer Bookman Old Style.

If you increase the font size for your chapter headings, and stay away from using the Heading 1 style, your book will be cleaner, your table of contents will function with minimal problems (I'll talk about the table of contents more in-depth in my next book about formatting), and the flow will be much better.

Paragraph Indents

-->You see this paragraph indent? Do yourself a favor and do that from your first paragraph. If your book has no paragraph indents, and the paragraphs are separated only by a line, it will look very amateurish and unprofessional.

Some writers prefer to use the full-block style for their first paragraph (meaning no indent in the first paragraph for each chapter), and that's fine, but if you want to upload your book to Smashwords for distribution to Apple, Overdrive, Barnes & Noble, etc., you'll get an autovetter error and have to go back in and make <u>all your paragraphs consistent</u>. After uploading a zillion times to Smashwords, believe me, I learned this the hard way. Pick a consistent style and stick with it.

Here is how you format if you want to use the formatting style I described above, using an indent:

Go to the 'Home' tab, and the 'Paragraph' section, click the small arrow on the right-hand side.

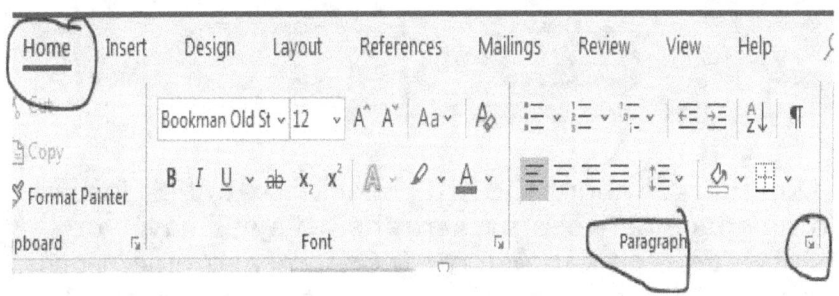

This is what you should select for your paragraph format:

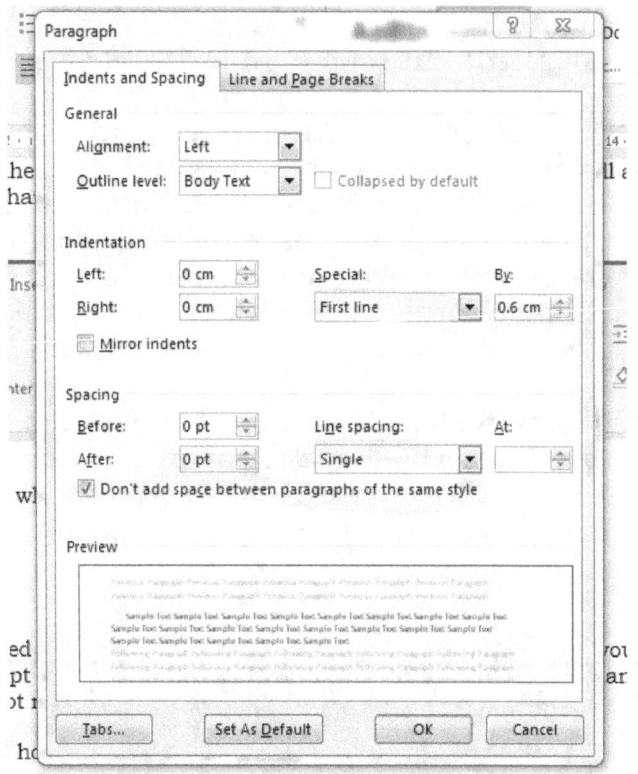

Don't forget about the little check box to tick for not adding space between paragraphs, this will save you lots of time. You can use the 0.6cm measurement or try another one if you want the indent to be bigger or smaller. I've used that size for all my books, and it seems to work.

I learned this the hard way. It takes hours to go back through your manuscript and insert your paragraph indents. It cannot be done any other way except manually, so I suggest you do it from the start.

This is how the manuscript <u>should</u> look:

Chapter 1

Sam cringed as he listened to the Peterson girls

fighting in the back room. He only knew one voice: his inside voice, and he couldn't compete with the noise; for this reason, he didn't intervene. Instead, he opened the DVD library under the television, and selected the girliest movie he could find. As he pushed the tape into the player and watched the screen come to life, he waited until the theme song came on, and turned the volume up as high as he could. Seconds later, both girls joined Sam on the couch, as they watched *Cinderella* for the hundredth time.

Lilian and Stephanie, the Peterson twins, were five years Sam's junior. Sam was the only twelve-year-old living on the block. For this reason, and only this reason, Sam was asked to sit for Mr. and Mrs. Peterson when they went to their weekly church meetings. Their Grampa, Mr. Seamington, made periodic visits on church nights. The man never smiled at Sam or talked to him directly. It bothered the young boy, but he babysat all the same, to respect his parents' wishes.

Stephanie Peterson had a small crush on Sam. He knew this because she would sit closest to him, and when the quiet boy spoke, she would stare at him, as though in awe. It had happened ever since the day Sam's long raven braid came out. The leather twine had given way, causing a wave of jet black, satiny hair to escape down his back. Sam's tribal name was 'Springwater'. His parents decided on Sam as a shorter version, to lessen the stigma when he began school.

Once your manuscript is finished, be sure to mirror all the above in your **back matter**, but we'll get to that in my next book.

Tools

We've already discussed using Word, and that's the only program I've ever used, and if it's good enough for me...some use other tools like Scrivener, and there are all sorts of other types of software out there, but I've always used Word and it's perfectly fine. I use a small laptop; it's actually a tablet with a keyboard attached, and it was given to me as a gift, so I pop that in my laptop bag and tote it with me to work each day.

The other tool I recommend is either a spare notepad (the old kind made of paper, not the app) and a pen or pencil to keep on you at all times, or the notes app on your cell phone. I'll get into why later. That's all you need to write a book.

Time

As the title says, you can write a book in as little as ten minutes a day, and it's true. If you have more time, great, or sometimes I get a chunk of more time to spare on the weekends, but not always. No matter what, if you have ten minutes a day, you can write a book. I promise.

How?

Focus and discipline. If you write for ten minutes (or more, if you have it) each day, every day, even on weekends, you'll get there.

Creating a Reference Document

If you have an idea for a book in mind; no matter what genre, no matter if it's fiction or non-fiction, I suggest you **type out all your ideas for the book first**. Every possible detail you can think of. It doesn't matter if it's a proper outline; I've never used one, just make sure you have everything on record that you want to include in the book, even if you don't use all the ideas, make sure you have them all typed up into a Word document, because this is the same document that you're going to use to write your book. You can even do it in point form if you want, just as long as you have your mind fresh and clear for when you start writing, so you can focus, and you're not finding yourself constantly going back to add necessary details you may have forgotten.

You'll find that you often reference this document, and add to it as well, as you go along. It can be a separate document, but it doesn't have to be. Whatever you find is easiest for you. Save your document and start writing your book at the top of the document, so your notes are on the bottom for easy reference. When you start writing, make sure you add character names, relationships to other characters, important points (ie. Birthdates, town names, Martin is in love with Phoebe, etc.) and details pertinent to the story that you may need to reference later. You'll also find this method handy when you're editing later, so you won't have to constantly scroll up and down in your manuscript, ensuring that you're referencing details accurately.

I've used both methods: creating a separate document entitled (for example), 'Don't Mess with Daddy's Girl – Character List', or simply leaving the document at the bottom of the manuscript. By creating a separate document, it is a little easier when you're editing after the manuscript is complete, since you don't have to scroll to the bottom each time you need to check something specific, but you can always create a separate document when you're editing by copying and pasting that information later, anyhow. Whatever works for you.

Here is an example of what I prepared for one of my novels (that I wrote in just ten minutes a day, by the way ;))

Notice how the grammar and **spelling is not correct**. These are just NOTES.

...

The Man with the Black Belt – Outline

Start off with a scene where the main character younger is babysitting a white female child. The grandfather is a racist and doesn't trust him. Somehow it turns out that the main character is accused of trying to touch the girl. The boy is shunned throughout the neighbourhood even though the parents do not press charges. There is never any evidence of wrongdoing or an investigation. Then, fast forward to the wedding....later the wife finds out what happened and uses it against the main character

3 parts:

Part 1:

A man is married to a very jealous women. He loves his son to bits but as he grows up and the marriage crumbles, his relationship with his son diminishes. The wife and son are jealous that the man spends so much time at the dojo and not with them. Eventually she leaves and threatens that if he wants to see the boy, that she will end his career by creating an untrue story of child abuse.

Part 2:

A young boy's parents are killed in a car crash and he is left to an orphanage. The first foster family they don't quite click; no abuse or neglect, just no real love between them. He runs away and somehow ends up in hospital where he bonds with a nurse, who ends up taking him home. She works long hours and he finds himself straying despite the strong love they have for each other. She herself is single, never married, no children...lonely and welcoming to a young boy who they have a lot in common with.

Part 3:

The boy has so much fear since witnessing something tramatic (think of something), he is mute, and shows much interest in a dojo. He watches them from the window for hours. The man sees him one day and asks him to come join them (the man is very soft spoken and gentle – he's aboriginal) and the boy finds him fascinating. When his new mother gets attacked one day, sensei saves her life using his fighting skills. The boy begins to speak after learning to keyei in class. At the end the man receives a humanitarian award and then his son comes to find him since he learned that his mother told him lies about his father.

...

And I didn't even use all this reference material. You'll find your book tends to take on a life of its own and it morphs and moulds into something else. Hence the additional notes that I added below the outline.

...

Sam is showing his 3 year old how to do kicks. He's graduated and working. becky is still in school in her last year. Sensei is showing signs of parkinson's or some other debilitating disease and cannot run the dojo. He asks sam to take over. It causes a brawl between him and bekcy. She desn't want the boy to do karate either. She wants sam to run her father's business instad

"Cut his balls off" *the boys laughed, turning a bloodied Sam over on his side, as he lay unconscious on the asphalt.* Do a montage like in Sandra Brown's book to illustrate how they beat him. He makes his speech for his humanitarian award, and admits that he began fighting in tournaments and won all over the world. Show that in the chapter where he and Becky marry; that his room is full of trophies that he received after he got his black belt. He wasn't motivated to fight until after the beating that nearly killed him. Show him fighting for his life in hospital and then fast forward to them going to college.

He's lucky to be able to have children since his one testicle had to be removed. Describe all the damage that Sam took when beaten, but his parents didn't press charges, partly because Sam doesn't tell them who did it or how it happened. He knows that sharing will only lead to another beating.

They find him balled up in the fetal position in the park. His bike is ruined, his backpack, wallet and money stolen. They don't press charges because they know it will only prompt another attack as the last one did.

Do a flashback later when he does a speech, recounting the attack that night. tell how they stuffed his mouth with a bandana soaked in alcohol so he couldn't yell for help. How they tackled him, five to one, and beat him, afterward leaving him for dead.

Add in his friend Peter from karate being a close friend; need more dimension. They go to the same school. He doesn't like Becky. His sister is autistic. Have it so Sam learns how to communicate with her.

Sam gets his black belt. He's seventeen and going away to college

Becky's birthday may 20
Sam's birthday July 7

Rick later becomes worse at breaking the law after stabbing Sam. Perhaps he's the one who comes back to seek vengeance later?

Two years later, Christopher's family is moving away. Both becky and sam go to the same high school. Both his older brothers have gone off to college. Sam is a quiet boy and decides to cut his hair, then the girls go wild and suddenly becky is all over him. They date and fall in love. Talk about him not being a traditional native, that's why she asked why he cut his hair. He gets his black belt and his entire family attends the ceremony. All the girls fawn over him but he's true to becky.

Add in a spot where sam protects lilian from a bully, but he screams "stop, I don't want any trouble!" and uses a pressure point instead of actual violence. He does it before her grampa sees but she does tell her mother. Mr. seamington never finds out.

...

Then at the bottom, I always list the character names and pertinent details for reference.

...

Gwen Peterson
Russell Peterson
Stephanie Peterson
Lillian Peterson (one with crush on Sam)
Jeffrey Seamington
Sam Corrolla
Desiree Corrolla
Reginald Corrolla
Max Corrolla
Tim Corrolla
Gregory Lindon
Marjorie Lindon
Brenda Lindon
Becky Lindon
Sensei Campbell
Shihan Groves
Sampai Hickson
Peter (another black belt)
Lucy (Peter's special needs sister)

How do you write for just ten minutes and accomplish something?

When I first started using this method, I thought, how on earth am I supposed to make a decent, quality novel, when my writing sessions are so short? I barely have time to get the idea down before I have to go back to work. I'll be honest, it does seem that way at first, but you'll find that even if you complete one paragraph, it's **progress.** You will be amazed how much you can write in ten minutes if you're <u>focused and if you practice</u>.

Hooking for the next writing session

You may be wondering how you just get started writing, and then you must stop, how you can continue the next time, without forgetting what you were writing to begin with. This was a common worry I had, until I learned to do my writing in spurts. If I know I have a large section to write, with lots of detail and dialogue, I jot down what I'm looking to get across (and it doesn't have to be grammatically perfect, either. As you saw in the example above, I typed willy-nilly, which is best). You will surprise yourself how easily words come out when you know exactly what you want to say.

This method I call '**hooking**'. Once I get my idea down for the next section, it's almost like anticipation; I can't wait to write it out the way I've set to do so, and then when I have that next ten minutes, the **words come out like lightning**. Try it. Trust me. After a while, you may not even have to take notes for what you plan on writing next; it may just pour out of you. That happens to me a lot. If you get stuck, read back a section or two. You'll get the feel for where you were going.

Review & Writer's Block

When you're having trouble figuring out where your book is going, or if you've hit an impasse in the storyline, don't give up, and don't set the manuscript down. I often find the beginning and the end of a book is the easiest part to write; it's the in-between that gets tough. Keep looking back at your outline and review the book from as far back as page one if you have to. Chances are, though, you'll only have to review a chapter or two to realize where you were going. Read through your notes, and if all else fails, just write.

The practice of writing itself will get your juices flowing. Think positive. Here are a few tips on how to get past writer's block:

- Take a nap
- Watch a movie
- Read a book
- Have a conversation with someone you haven't spoken to in a while
- Get out of the house!

Any of those ideas will help get your creativity flowing again. And sometimes, when you least expect it, an idea will pop into your mind. That is why you always need to carry your pen and paper or notes app around with you. As fast as an idea pops into your head, it may get lost, so write it down immediately!

One Halloween, I was in the middle of writing '**Don't Mess with Daddy's Girl**', a suspense novel, and, although I wasn't quite at an impasse, I was in the middle of a chapter that wasn't really coming together with enough punch, and I wasn't sure how to kick up the suspense a notch. That was the day our Fire Department was holding a fundraiser for a local charity by making the fire hall into a Haunted Mansion. As we stood in line for our kids to have a go at it, we watched a little girl cower away from the line, in fear of the setup. One of the firemen came over, crouched down, and spoke to her so softly and so poignantly that it nearly brought tears to my eyes when she suddenly took the man's hand and went through the scary house.

At that moment, a childhood memory was triggered for me, giving me a perfect way to end my chapter, and I also came up with another idea for my book, proudly titled '**She Only Speaks to Butterflies**'. As we were driving home from the fire hall, I was feverishly typing notes into my phone with ideas for that next book. So, trust me, getting out of the house helps!

Fortunately, if you follow this method, I can guarantee you will most likely **never have writer's block**. Over time, your mind will be trained to write, and you'll always have an idea in mind to write next. The problem is sometimes ideas come flowing too quickly into your brain. Ideas for your next book, for example. That is also why it is vital to carry around a pen and paper or your phone, so you can harness all that creative energy.

This book (that you're currently reading) was an idea that I've had for years. I know that there are so many authors and to-be authors out there who just can't find the time to write. And I truly believe that if I can find the time, anyone can. I have a full-time, forty hour a week job, a mortgage, a husband, two small children, a house, and two cats. If I can write a book in ten minutes a day, so can you!

Tense and POV

Another important factor to know before you begin writing, is what tense to use. In the beginning, I used first-person present tense. At that time, I was thinking of pursuing an agent, and after some research, I learned that most agents look for third-person past tense. To save yourself some trouble, please decide what route you would like to go with your writing. It is extremely difficult and frustrating to re-rewrite a manuscript, whatever length, in a different tense and point of view. Believe me, I've had to do it...more than once.

If you're thinking of pursuing an agent, or even if you want to pursue small press publishing, do your homework and find out what tense and POV (point of view) they prefer. I have had to do the unfavourable deed of going back and changing an entire manuscript after learning that the agent I wanted to pursue preferred different tense and POV than what I had written.

The flip-side is if you want to self-publish. You must determine what voice <u>you</u> want in order to make your story the most effective. Also, what writing techniques you want to use. Sometimes you don't know which ones in the beginning, and you can change them as you go along, but it's best to <u>know before you start</u>.

In case you're unsure of what POV exists, here is a brief recap and explanation of each:

- First-person present tense (ie. I am watching my dog lay on the blanket)
- First-person past tense (ie. I watched the dog lay on the blanket)
- Third-person present tense (ie. She watches her dog lay on the blanket)
- Third-person past tense (ie. She watched her dog lay on the blanket)

Writing Techniques

Different writing techniques also work better for other storylines. For example, you can use flashbacks, diary-style writing (Gone Girl), montages, add different parts to your story to delineate it between characters, or you can just write naturally and not use any styles, if it is more fitting.

One of my favourites is the montage. I'd never seen it anywhere until I read one of Sandra Brown's latest novels and thought that it was just brilliant. In the novel I just finished before starting this book, titled '**The Man with the Black Belt**', I used it to advance the main character's lifetime by about three years. You can use other methods, like going from spring to fall and describing the landscape or use a pregnant character who has then had her baby, etc., but I thought the montage worked best because I wanted to describe certain events within a timeline, without going into great detail.

Here is an example:

"I didn't really want to watch a movie; that was just a cover. Let's hit the pub up the street and chat for a while. Is that cool?"

Sam knew exactly what was on Peter's mind.

Five minutes later they arrived at The Squire and Firken pub. Ten minutes later they'd made a decision that would change both their lives forever.

...

"Are you going to keep the name of the dojo? Oh my God, Sam! This is so exciting! I can't wait for Michael to grow up so he can understand what his daddy does for a living!"

...

"Daddy, do I have to go to school? I want to come with you to the dojo."

"No, Michael. I know you've been coming with daddy to the dojo for a while, but it's time for you to start Junior Kindergarten. You can still come after school. Daddy and all the kids will still have classes at night."

"Can you show me a proper roundhouse kick?"

Sam chuckled. "Yes, love. Daddy can teach you whatever you want."

...

"Sam, I think we have to forget about the World Championships this time around again. Lisa and I get married in a couple of months and I can't afford to travel when my wife-to-be wants to honeymoon in Puerto Rico."

Sam smirked. "Ah, dump her."

"You dump your wife first, dude."

"Hey, I have a child."

"You are a child. I don't know how Becky puts up with you."

"I'm her bodyguard."

"Michael's her bodyguard."

...

"Sam! Sam! Wake up! You're having a nightmare!" Becky hissed. "It's okay, Sam. It's me. I'm here." She pushed a lock of hair away from his face. His ponytail had come loose; a pool of hair surrounded his pillow.

Sam awoke with a start. "Honey, it's okay. I'm here." She soothed.

His body shivered with fear. He was soaked; sweat dripped from his forehead. Becky turned and pulled the cord on the lamp. The bedroom illuminated with a soft light. "Jesus, Sam, are you okay? Do you need some water or something?"

Sam was humiliated. Almost twenty-two years old and he was still suffering from nightmares. "I'm fine."

Becky sobbed, stroking his forehead. "No, you're not fine. Sam, please," she begged. "Tell me what's troubling you."

Sitting up straight in bed, Sam raked a hand through his hair.

"Sam we've been married almost five years and you've always had these dreams." She took his hand in hers. "Tell me. Please tell me what they're about."

Looking at his wife's pleading expression, Sam relented. After a few moments he found his voice. "They're about the times I was attacked." He explained softly, as if the dream would return if he spoke too loudly about it. "Sometimes they're about that old man that lives up the street. Mr. Seamington. But mostly I see Christopher's face in my dreams. And sometimes it's Rick, the guy who stabbed me. The odd time I can still feel the pain and see the damage like it all happened yesterday."

Becky continued to stroke his hand, listening intently. "They went away for a while after Michael was born."

"I know." Becky glided her hand across Sam's exposed stomach, touching his scars. He didn't flinch even though she'd never really touched him in those areas before. His shorts were lopsided in his underwear area, where the last vicious attack left him with only one testicle. She caressed his private area, as though through her touch, she could heal him. It wasn't a sexual touch; neither responded in kind. "It's a miracle that Michael was conceived." She said after a beat. "It's a miracle you lived, let alone that we were able to make a child of our own."

Do you see how this method would work? I just wanted to leave tiny breadcrumbs leading into what will happen next, not full scenes.

Although self-explanatory, here is an example of a flashback from the book I referenced above, titled '**She Only Speaks to Butterflies**':

Chapter 3

"Knock knock!" Sarah sang from the other side of the porch door. "I brought goodies!"
Sarah's swelling belly was covered with a sweaty t-shirt. It looked like paper mache pasted on an oversized balloon. Her belly button was beginning to protrude. She waddled her way in through the unlocked screen door. The cotton skirt nearly caught in the doorframe.
"We're just up here!" Sherry called from the second floor.
"You want some tea?" Sarah asked, opening the cabinet door above the sink. Her short ponytail bobbed every time she moved.
"Sure." Sherry sauntered down the steps, pulling her unruly brown curls into a bun on top of her head. "I just finished bathin' Denise. She's up there playin' while her hair dries."
Sherry peeked out of the curtains on her kitchen

door, pressing her ample chest against the cool wood. "Where's Mark?"

"Oh honey, he's watchin' some sports thang on television." Sarah stuck her index finger in her mouth and made a face, feigning a gag. Her long fingernails nearly reached the back of her throat. "I don't know what makes me more nauseous, the smell of anchovies on his damn pizza or the sound of thousands of angry sports fans howlin' at the crappy players."

Glancing at her best friend's newly colored red hair, Sherry's face twisted into a smile.

"At least they have nice behinds," Sarah added.

Sherry blushed. "Did Mark even notice ya left?"

Sarah filled the kettle with water.

"He'll notice when he runs outta chips."

"Why? Doesn't he know where you keep 'em?"

Sarah took a sugar square out of the container on the counter and popped it into her mouth.

"He'll notice because there ain't any left." She pointed at herself proudly. "I ate 'em."

Giving her an evaluating glance, Sherry commented. "Girl, how have ya not gained a hundred pounds? God, when I was carryin' Denise, I drank *water* and got fat."

Sarah waved like it was nothing. "I work it off."

"What, at the salon? You gettin' busier lately?" Sherry tucked a loose curl behind her ear.

"Huh! Are you kiddin' me?" Sarah yelled. "Mary barely lets me lift a finger around there." She tutted. "Na, it's my hormones. Me and Mark have sex like twice a night. The sweaty kind, ya know?" her face scrunched.

"Really?" Sherry's brow rose, filling the tea pot and pouring two mugs full. "God, I faked sleep all the time when I was carryin' Denise."

"Mark tries. But if he ain't snoring..."

Sherry almost spat a mouthful of tea out. "I gotta go check on Denise." Her face was red.

A little while later Sherry came back downstairs, having changed into a short cotton house dress. "Out like a light."

"Must be the medicine." Sarah offered, and then changed the subject. "So, did ya hear about the new hospital comin'?"

"Yeah, Kate mentioned it earlier."

"I was kinda hopin' it would be built before junior here arrives, but I don't see that happenin' unless they do an express build."

"Come on, it takes sometimes years to build somethin' like that. You'll be workin' on your second before that's finally erected."

"So did Kate tell you where it was going to be?"

Sherry leaned her chin on her hand. "Apparently the jury's still out on that."

Sarah shook her head, as if preparing to argue. "Now listen, I love ya honey, but regardless of what happens with that damn hospital, it's time to move on." Sarah rubbed her stomach and Sherry watched it twitch slightly as the baby moved around. "Now, Ned and Kate made me keep it from ya for this long, but it's not healthy." She stopped to take a sip of tea. "For Denise or for you."

Lifting her head off her hand, Sherry looked speculatively at Sarah. "What do ya suggest I do? It's not that easy to forget."

Sarah lowered the leg she had dangling off the side of the chair. "I'm not askin' you to forget. That's impossible. But as your best friend, I'm tellin' ya it's time to start thinkin' 'bout the future, not the past."

They sat and sipped their tea for a minute in silence.

"You still in therapy?" Sarah asked.

"You know I am," Sherry answered flatly.

"Good. Stay in it." Sarah rose and walked to the entrance door. She slipped the set of keys off the hook with her long fingernail and passed them to Sherry. "Go for a drive. I'll stay here with Denise. It'll be fine."

Sherry looked down at her hand and clasped her keys gently. "I'm not sure I'm ready yet. Don't I get time to think about this?"

Sarah lifted her arms. "So if yer not ready, yer not

ready," she insisted. "There's only one way to find out."

...

His hands were interlaced in hers as she pushed the stroller with one hand down the boardwalk. Seagulls soared overhead and dive-bombed down as Denise screeched with glee, grasping her half-melted cherry popsicle in one hand, and her Elmo doll in the other. "Mommy! Birds!" she pointed excitedly.

Chris playfully shoved Sherry away so he could push the carriage. Sherry watched him race her around. Denise laughed so hard she dropped her popsicle.

Sherry hollered. "She should have been a boy!"

"Maybe next time." Chris shrugged, slowing the stroller. "We live in a small town." His index finger was on his chin as if in deep thought. "We'll have five more...one of 'em is bound to be a boy."

"Are you serious?" Sherry blurted. "You want to have six kids?"

"I'm a lawyer." Chris buffed his nails on his shirt. "We can afford it."

"Mommy? How come butterflies are so much prettier than seagulls?" Denise asked, watching the birds fly overhead.

Chris interrupted from behind. "Because butterflies pollinate the pretty flowers and seagulls just eat fish...and...other stuff." He said cautiously, sensing his wife's glare.

Denise smiled at Chris. "Can I have a butterfly?"

"You mean...for a pet?" Chris asked. "We'll see." He closed one eye and put his index finger on his nose. "Maybe Daddy will get ya a special one that can live in yer bedroom."

Denise beamed. "A purple one."

"I'll see what I can do."

Sherry's reverie was broken by a car honking behind her. She'd come to a full stop but didn't signal, like she was indecisive about her next move. The frustrated driver rolled past and then she turned into the abandoned strip of road ahead.

The orange and black-checkered road closure sign was slightly bent and hanging off to the side from the bad storm the previous year. Sherry parked next to the sign and froze, recounting a conversation.

"In this small town, we're worth more dead than alive, Sherry," Chris mused.

"Don't talk like that, honey. You made vows to me and I to you. We're not allowed to leave each other." Her finger was pointing at him the way her mother used to point at her when she'd misbehaved as a child.

"Seriously. Why do you have to have such a big insurance policy, anyway? Yer only twenty five."

"I'm a lawyer, sweetie." His tone changed. "I see people left with nothin' every day. I won't see my family suffer like that."

"So why don't we enjoy some of the money we have now? Why do we have to scrimp and save like this all the time? We have more money in our savings than my parents had their entire lives."

"If we want a big family, we need to plan," he said simply. "This house is small and we'll be trippin' over each other after two or three." He cleared his throat. "The housin' market here is slim and if we need a bigger house, it's goin' to cost us a lot. We need to save for it now."

"Alright. But we're redecoratin' Denise's room this week. You promised," she warned.

"That's right, Daddy, you promised," Denise said, entering the room, carrying a stuffed purple butterfly.

Chris lifted her into his lap. "And let me guess how you'd like it decorated..." He looked down at her plush toy. "With butterflies?"

Denise's face lit up. "Can I?"

"I don't see why not."

Sherry pulled up beside the ditch and cut the engine. She looked into the sky and was welcomed with twilight. The clouds were deep purple and the sun was trying to peek at her from behind the horizon, glaring into her deep blue eyes. Trees were waving slowly with the light spring breeze and she swore she heard a voice flowing by her ear, whispering to her.

Looking at the desolate area she got a chill down her spine. Every time she visited, it refreshed her memory of one of the most horrific moments in her life. Masochistically, she kept coming back.

"Take Denise and go get help," Chris insisted. "I don't want her to see me like this."

"But I can't leave you," she sobbed. "You're bleedin'."

The gash above his left temple was slowly trickling blood down his face, leaving a line that looked like a valley on a road map.

"Sherry, we're not far from the Baker's farm. Go, take Denise and run for help. Ned and Kate will know what to do."

Sherry looked back at her daughter, sobbing so hard she had hiccups. The driver's side door frame was wedged up against Chris's skull, preventing him from moving.

He winced. "I need you to go now, Sherry. I need help; I'm slippin' away."

Quickly, Sherry lifted herself up, cursing her husband for taking a detour. As she opened the door, it creaked. The tree that had fallen on the car still dangled from its roots. Sherry opened the passenger side door and scooped her shaken daughter from the vehicle.

"I love you. I'll be right back," she told Chris and began running, as fast as she could, towards Baker's farm.

Looking up at the gravel path she could almost see her harried footprints from that day. Her feet barely touched the ground she ran so fast, holding Denise in her arms, scarcely aware of how heavy she was.

When they returned in Ned Baker's pickup truck, Sherry instructed Denise to stay in the vehicle. Chris's head lay on the side of the door, leaning lazily, as though he was rested at a stop light. Something was different; his eyes were open but unfocused. Sherry let out a loud shriek.

To her horror, Denise walked over to the side of the car and climbed under the tree trunk. She stood, staring at her father's lifeless body, seemingly unaware that he was dead. The young woman watched her daughter hold out her hand while a purple butterfly landed on her finger, perching with its wings intermittently swaying in and out. She called out to Denise but the child was silent...she had remained silent ever since.

Sherry ran her hand along the sign and glanced over at the sawed-off tree trunk, the only thing that changed since the accident. The town decided to close that road indefinitely, it had always been a dangerous detour that Ned and Kate tried to get closed for years, knowing some day it would be the cause of someone's demise.

Chris was buried in the town cemetery, but she could never bring herself to visit. Her mother-in-law turned it into some floufy-coufy miniature garden, where she always had a candle lit and a picture of him as a boy enshrined in the background. It gave her the creeps. This little sanctuary was hers. She didn't change it except for the wreath she placed at the face of the tree trunk.

Her wedding band, still hugging her finger after all, was a constant reminder. It made her feel married; she liked that. Their wedding picture never left her purse since his death nearly two years ago.

Tires were crackling down the gravel road as Sherry lifted her head, drying her tears. Ned Baker smiled apologetically as he approached. He spoke gently.

"Sorry love, Sarah's been worried about ya. Personally, I think she's just hungry and I know you ain't got the best food supply over there." He watched Sherry smile thinly and added "Come on, hop in. I'll get your car home to ya later, love."

See how I used italics to delineate between the

flashback and the regular prose? Lovin' that!
   There are other writing techniques out there, but these are the most common, I think. Try a few...don't be afraid!

Time and Repetition

   To get your story flowing nicely, you'll need to establish a regimen of <u>writing every day</u>. Every day during my lunch I write, and sometimes a little in the evening if there is spare time. Weekends I also try to squeeze some time in there, but not always. If we're going on a road trip, I bring my laptop and utilize that time as well. Also, some of the evening and weekend time I save for marketing and promotion, such as blogging, making new Twitter/Facebook posts, and generally reviewing where my sales are, and what I can do to increase them. So, basically, the majority of my writing time is the ten or fifteen minutes I have to spare after I've eaten my lunch.
   Repetition works very well for me. In fact, it doesn't matter when I write, as long as I do a little each day. This way the work is still fresh, no matter what happened the previous day. I almost don't have to make notes if I write every day.

What do you do when your book is done?

   There are so many things to do once your book is complete, that one may think writing the book is the easy part. In many respects, it is. One thing I always do though, when my book is done...is **celebrate**. Whether it be indulging in a dessert treat, watching a movie, or buying myself something new, it is important to rejoice in some way. Also, very important...spread the news! Post it all over social media, blog about it, let everyone know that the work you've set out to do is finally complete.

You don't have to reveal too much about the storyline (in fact, I recommend that you don't), but give a one-liner for the premise of the book.

Start Writing Your Next Book

Especially if you're a series writer, or you want to be. I never release a book in a series without being finished the next one in the series. That link in the back matter is what drives sales for the next book, and can potentially lead to huge pre-orders, so don't let your readers down! They'll be waiting to read your next book if they enjoy the one you're releasing now! **One small caveat**: never put a book up for pre-order *unless your first draft is complete*. That's a personal rule I have, because if you don't finish your book in time, you're in a heap of doo-doo with vendors.

The Lull

To be clear, the 'lull' doesn't imply writer's block. When I refer to a lull, it's more of a break to do other things. I hit a lull with this book recently, when I had to put together materials and things to launch my completed manuscript into a Kindle Scout campaign. Taking about three weeks to edit and re-edit, as well as prepare materials, I couldn't touch this book for a few weeks. Once I got back into it, I had to read it all over again to remember what point I was at. This was actually a good thing, because it triggered a whole bunch of other things that I wanted to add. I wrote it in the bottom of my notes and carried on.

This part being 'the lull' was what I added but reading through your material does help to initiate the creative process. One thing that can also trigger a lull is when you forget something. Whether it's the name of something or something that you wanted to reference from earlier in the book, that maybe you forgot to put in your notes. What I do in this case is put notes in a bracket in the spot where I can't come up with the idea and add it in later i.e.. (Sam's school name), or (month Sam was born). You get the idea. This keeps the writing process flowing.

Back Matter

In case you're unsure of what back matter is, it's what you choose to put in your book after the story is finished. Most authors put their backlist (books that you have already published - if you have any), a preview of the next book (if it's a series), or the next standalone novel or newest release. I also add in a review request and author's note. How you choose to add these is up to you.

Some authors put the covers to their books in their back matter, but I wouldn't advise this for three reasons: 1) covers get updated. The last thing you want is to have to update all the back matter for all your books when you change a cover. 2) sometimes the images are too small, and they are pixelated (plus, your delivery fee may increase the more images you have in your book. 3) it can look too busy. I once clumped all my book covers that were part of a series in order (putting all the books in a series together), and it looked awful.

My advice is to just **list your books**. If you want, include the cover for the next release or the next book in the series. But again, I don't advise it. What I do advise you to do is to place a newsletter signup link, a link directly to your website, and a concise description (or blurb) of your next book. I also sometimes put in the first chapter of my next book, but not usually.

Editing

The nice thing about reviewing your work frequently is that you can edit as you go along. Many writers/editors say that this is a no-no, because it can stilt the writing process, but I don't believe this to be true. Not only does it refresh your memory so you can remember what you last wrote, but it also enables you to make small edits, so it isn't a huge undertaking when the manuscript is complete. The only way that it stifles your writing, is if you go through and re-write scenes that don't necessarily need to be re-written. Doing that once or twice in a whole manuscript is okay, but don't get hooked on that, as it will deconstruct your work, and cause you to be tempted to throw the whole thing out! Don't do it!

One thing that helped me a lot when I first started writing, was **Stephen King's book 'On Writing'** Fair warning: I do mention it a lot in the rest of this book. He suggests leaving your manuscript for a minimum of a month before editing (I think he suggests three months, but I just couldn't wait that long). The key here is to start a new manuscript in the interim. This way, after a month or so, your original manuscript will be fresher, and it will almost seem like an entirely different book from when you last worked on it. You'll be able to spot holes in the story, grammar and spelling mistakes, and inconsistencies, a lot easier.

Paying for editing is something I'll argue over. In the beginning, yes, it's inconceivable to self-publish or submit an unedited manuscript to an agent. But for me, after spending upwards of two thousand dollars on a spotty editing job, by a reputable editor (referred by a reputable author), and having readers point out mistakes in unfavourable reviews, I've since been very hesitant about paid editing. I did use two other editors for other works, but still found mistakes and had unfavourable reviews. It seems the books that were self-edited (and I say this with a heavy-hand, I'll explain later) seem to get better reviews and no complaints about editing.

Don't beat yourself up about the odd spelling or grammatical error. I'm a huge Sandra Brown fan, and many of her books I've found obvious errors in. So, if she does it, I suppose everybody does. I'll talk about this later, but once you're well on your way with readers, ask a handful of them to pre-read or beta read your book before publication. You'll be amazed at how well these typo-hunters can pick out all the errors.

Run your book through Word's spellcheck (although Word does highlight potential errors throughout your work – pay attention and review them as you go along) and use the same idea for letting your book 'stew' for a while. Once you go back and re-read it, you'll see different mistakes.

Reading your book aloud (like I learned painfully in recent weeks when I attempted to record my first audiobook), this points out lots of errors with grammar, flow and you'd be surprised how many spelling errors you'll find when you read your book out loud. Also, try reading it to someone, they can help point out what sounds odd, and it could be something that you didn't even catch.

10 Common Mistakes Made in Your First Draft

After having my second romance novel professionally edited, I thought it would be neat to keep the original draft and compare the two to see what common mistakes were made. I thought by sharing them, it might help those currently working on a manuscript to avoid these mistakes or to look out for them when editing.

1. Incorrect placement of quotation marks. My quotation marks were put *before* the period in most of my dialogue. They belong <u>after</u>. Your sentence needs to end before the quotation mark.

    <u>Wrong</u>: "Oh, honey, it's not your fault".

Right: "Oh, honey, it's not your fault."

2. Capitalizing 'he said' or she said' at the end of dialogue. This is self-explanatory, but I'll give an example.

   Wrong: "Oh, honey, it's not your fault." She said.

   Right: "Oh, honey, it's not your fault." she said.

3. Using a period instead of a comma within the dialogue. This gets tricky. If the dialogue is complete and the thought has ended, then you would use a period, but my common mistake was using a period in each case.

   Wrong: "Good evening, Sarah's." she greeted cheerfully.
       "It's me." I said, trying to stifle a sniffle.

   Right: "Good evening, Sarah's," she greeted cheerfully.
       "It's me," I said, trying to stifle a sniffle.

4. The semi-colon vs. period vs. comma argument. This was probably my most common mistake. When I should have used a period, I used a semi-colon, and where is should have used a period, I used a comma.

   Wrong:

   "He sounded weird and said I better come home; that he wasn't feeling well."

   Right:

"He sounded weird and said I better come home, that he wasn't feeling well."

Wrong:

"I've got a meeting at school today. Preparation for September; it's only five weeks away you know."

Right:

"I've got a meeting at school today. Preparation for September. It's only five weeks away you know."

Wrong:

"It's delicious...the guys will like it too, did you make lots?"

Right:

"It's delicious...the guys will like it too. Did you make lots?"

5. Whether to use the comma or period before dialogue. I always used the period or nothing where I should have used the comma.

Wrong:

I asked the inevitable question "Can I see him?"

Right:

I asked the inevitable question, "Can I see him?"

6. To break up a sentence with a comma or period or not. I had trouble deciding on the flow of some

sentences, so I mostly threw in a comma for good measure. Wrong. My best advice is to read the sentence out loud. If you have to take a breath to finish the sentence, it likely needs a comma (or period).

<u>Wrong</u>:

I knew Jennifer couldn't handle this; she had just broken up with her first boyfriend, so I thought it best to wait.

<u>Right</u>:

I knew Jennifer couldn't handle this, she had just broken up with her first boyfriend, so I thought it best to wait.

7. Starting a new paragraph when needed. I would continue dialogue in the same paragraph when I should have begun a new one.

<u>Wrong</u>:

My eyes followed Mark as he came closer to me, looking at me suspiciously. He played along, "Really? A luscious meal huh...what's this about good fortune? I didn't play the lotto today." I shook my head, "No, it said *my* good fortune." He nodded and his eyebrows rose. "Yeah, but your good fortune is *half* mine, right?"

<u>Right</u>:

My eyes followed Mark as he came closer to me, looking at me suspiciously.
He played along, "Really? A luscious meal huh...what's this about good fortune? I didn't play the lotto today."

I shook my head, "No, I said *my* good fortune."
He nodded and his eyebrows rose, "Yeah, but your good fortune is *half* mine, right?"

8. Repetition. For some reason I liked saying 'winked' a lot after dialogue, or 'she looked at him like he had two heads', or the worst ones were constant crying or referring to people being late: 'he texted her to say he would be late', or she would be late for dinner again tonight. When you see a theme being repeated, switch it up or delete it.

9. Improper use of description. For example, after dialogue 'she returned', or 'she offered', when simply 'she said' would have sufficed.

10. Using too many words. This is a tough one when it's your first draft, because we tend to let the words flow out (which we should when it's our first draft, as that's the best way to get your ideas out). Just remember to go back and cut the fat.

Wrong: We lay in bed together the whole night, making love for many hours, so glad to be united forever.
Right: We lay in bed the whole night, making love for many hours. (the scene would have already eluded to a wedding, so the last piece would have been repetitive).

Creating a Main Character Readers Will Love to Hate

When we create controversial characters in stories, we often use them simply for background; to highlight a scene or subplot, or to bring a challenge to another character.

But what about using a bad boy or bad girl as a <u>main character</u>? How does that change things?

Creating a bad boy main character has been done so many times, this is where you need to pull out your entire writer's toolbox and invent a character so different that readers will look at him and wonder how you came up with him.

For example, in one of my novels **The Wheels of Change**, I made the bad boy character an invalid. Of course, he didn't start out that way, but it's his predicament that forces him to change for the better. The novel begins with him as a womanizing, egotistical, rich advertising executive, but he sleeps with the wrong woman and then finds himself behind the wheel of a vehicle without brakes. His experience living in a wheelchair is what transforms him into the wholesome, caring and humble person he becomes.

It's important to inject enough character development in the beginning (and possibly the middle) of the story to make the reader hate the main character before the transition begins to occur. Almost every other character in the novel must hate him, too, and have plenty of reasons to. It's almost as if the reader and the secondary characters need to join an 'I hate this guy' clique. The 'clique' and its purpose should almost be as strong as the character.

Once you have everybody on board, hating this guy, that's when the magic happens. If you can accomplish this, you're halfway there. The other half is in the pacing of the transition. If you're too fast about having the 'bad guy' (or girl) character transpire into a good person, it will come across fake or unrealistic. Alternatively, if you take it too slow, your readers may lose interest.

When your main character is controversial, there must be an overarching incident that causes the transition to commence; but be careful not to make that your primary climax. If you want to make the transition from bad to good very strong and life-changing, then that must be at least part of the climax.

The moment of catharsis, the epiphany or that scene where the main character realizes the meaning of life, must happen right before the climax. That's what will make the reader fall out of hate and fall in love with the main character.

Why it's so important to write as yourself

Let me clarify. When I write my novels, I'm always writing from someone else's perspective and with someone else's reactions, personality, etc.

Have you ever asked yourself after reading a book "I wonder what the writer is like?" Most authors do write a little from themselves in each character, however, the mystified reader will want to know what the writer is like outside of the world of fiction.

Therefore, when we write blogs, interviews, etc., it is my opinion that we should always write as our self. Don't sanitize your piece to say what you think others will want you to say or to cater to some other thought or person; write as yourself.

The way I do this is to pretend that I'm writing the piece for my best friend. That way my work will be honest, respectful and succinct. When you write this way, it is a no-holds-barred kind of conversation you'll have with yourself...and your audience. And that's what makes writing truly unique.

Writers often write too professionally in my opinion. I'm guilty of doing this in the past (especially since I'm a business major). Truthfully, after having read hundreds of other people's work, I've realized that the most interesting pieces were those that were written in a completely 'naked' manner. Reading is more enjoyable when there are no thought preambles or explanations, just the simple truth; where the reader can make their own assumptions. No spoon-feeding jargon, no words conjured up to impress, just simple, honest words.

Stephen King alluded to this in his book 'On Writing',

he basically suggested that if a word fits, use it. Don't choose a bigger word to impress; if the word 'late' works, don't use 'tardy' (unless you've already used 'late' and it will be repetitive). Proofreading aloud works well for this method, too. After completing your work, read it to yourself or to someone else. If it rolls naturally off your tongue, then you know you've chosen the right words and you're using your natural voice.

What do you do When You're Stuck Writing a Scene?

Some writers get stuck coming up with a book idea, a title or any other major part of their masterpiece. My major issue is getting stuck writing a scene. Here's a simple technique I use to stop writer's block and keep the work flowing.

<u>First and most importantly</u>: **don't stop writing**.

I use a free-for-all writing technique where I simply write the problem scene, no matter how flat, silly or relevant it is. I write and then make notes at the bottom as to what the purpose of the scene should be.

Then I take a break, get a snack or do something else (use your discretion in the amount of time away-just don't leave it for more than a day or you're more likely to give up). I don't think about the scene at all. When I come back, I read the chapter before the problem scene, then the problem scene that I wrote earlier, and my notes.

Ninety percent of the time I'll come up with a much better way to write the scene or edit it so it reads as it should. It works for me and it's much better than simply giving up and shelving your work.

Tip: break the scene up. One of the best ways to get stuck in a scene is by putting too much importance and/or action in it.

In the last scene of my book ***The Wife of a Lesser Man***, I wanted to give the reader an important message:

that the main character had forgiven his wife and whatever happened in the course of the book; all that mattered was that she was okay and that they could move on. I wanted to show the unconditional love he still had for her.

This placed way too much importance on the scene, making it too difficult to write. Instead, I reflected the main character's feelings throughout the last part of the book. Meaningful dialogue was added to different scenes in the latter half of the story. The message was delivered much better in the end and it made the scene almost like the last word; like the icing on the cake.

Writing a scene involves so many elements, but once you've written hundreds of them, you'll realize that with practice, naturally you'll get better. Just keep writing those scenes; never give up and always believe that you'll get it perfect with a little perseverance, faith and of course, patience.

Five Key Elements to Writing a Gripping Story

Character Development - Meaning that you have to help the reader get to know your characters. Get the reader to like them, too. It's not enough just to acquaint. You have to hook them in, so that when the story begins to unfold, you keep their interest. Make the reader care about the people telling your story, or the reader will not care about the story, either.

Romance Tip: In romance, it's not enough to develop the story for each individual character, you also need to develop the romantic arc itself. You can't simply have two people who lead interesting lives, and just mix them up together, making them fall in love. To have a powerful romance, you have to build it. Decide what kind of romance you want to create: slow burn, instant sizzle, etc., and build based on that pace.

Interesting Characters - It's not enough to just have characters. That's a given that a book has to have people in them to tell the story. They have to be exciting via elements within their lives. If you tell a story about boring people, then the story itself will be boring, unless, of course, the story is what makes them un-boring, ie....There is a lesson in there somewhere that makes the character more interesting, that's different.

A Villain - For me, every story has to have some sort of villain or evil behind it somewhere. This helps to shape the characters. It gives them a challenge. It also gives balance to the book. If you have all sunshine and roses, then the story will be too sweet and less interesting. Especially if it's a romance. I think sometimes the villains are as important as the main characters in a romance, because they tend to bring out the romantic arc more by creating more closeness with the characters' relationship.

A Lesson or a Challenge - This goes hand in hand with having a villain. It's about balance. Creating a story that has no impact will do just that. This is the part where you can sprinkle a little bit of wisdom in your story. Help the reader learn something. Take something that you're good in (or can research) and add in that element. It can be anything from travelling to a different country, overcoming illness (mental/physical), etc. Some of the lessons I've used in my stories are: mental illness, drug abuse, alcoholism, physical deformity, PTSD, the list goes on.

Cliffhanger Chapter Endings - This is something really cool that I picked up on when reading the Fifty Shades trilogy. E.L. James mastered this, and I use it frequently, too. To keep the reader turning the pages, don't end the chapter. Leave a scene hanging so the reader has to read on to find out what happens. The cliffhanger ending to a book is a little bit different, in that you work the storyline up to a climax, but leave the ending as a hook, so the reader is left wondering what is going to happen next.

Bonus: Make it Realistic and Relatable - Depending on taste, a reader may strive for a book that is true-to-life, or fantasy. Personally, I can't get past a novel that I can't relate to. Which is why you'll never catch me reading (or writing) fantasy or science fiction. Some romance readers often look for something completely off the wall, too, and as a writer, you must decide what market you are targeting. In my opinion, it's best to shoot for your own taste. For me, after reading a handful of romances that were so farfetched, I couldn't stomach the thought, and I vowed to make my books as realistic as possible. No fake boyfriends, husbands, anything like that. That's my creative edge and what my readers enjoy. It says so right in my tagline: Love stores that could actually happen. But again, it's all in what your taste is. Just be careful to create a story that is remotely realistic/relatable, unless it's satire or something clearly written on the label. **Give your readers what you say you're going to give them.**

The First Paragraph

The first paragraph, and really, the **first line**, are critical to your book, which is why I'm mentioning this now, as I didn't want to stilt your writing process or put too much pressure on you. What I do, unless I come up with a really killer first liner for my book, is <u>write it last</u>. That first line is almost as important as your blurb and hook. In fact, technically, it's another hook. The first paragraph should complement your first paragraph and lead the reader into the story successfully. Then follow through with a catchy first chapter, one that gives snippets of what's going to happen throughout the whole book. The first chapter should set the stage for everything.

Once you're versed in writing that first paragraph and first chapter, it'll be second nature to you. But you should keep that consistency throughout the book. Use the cliffhanger chapter endings that we just discussed to keep your readers' attention. And remember that for Amazon, the **'Look Inside' feature** allows readers to view usually the first five chapters of a novel (depending on how many words it is – and it changes, too). So make sure that those chapters **make the reader committed to the rest of the book**, also, ensure that the book is consistent throughout. What I mean by that is don't have the first five chapters with a lot of action or gripping suspense, and then none in the middle, and then throw some in the end for good measure. Make the book chock full of good stuff!

Here are a few of my first paragraphs from the first in series books (that are permanently free on all retailers, by the way, so if you ever want to pick one up and take a gander at what I'm talking about, go ahead!)

From 'No More Tears' (Sandy Appleyard)

They all stare at the floor with their Stetsons laying in their laps, as I chide them, one-by-one. The rickety, wooden chairs are lined up, a foot apart, like a set of dominoes, and none of the men dares to move.

"It belonged to my mother." I continue, using a curt tone I don't often use with my ranch hands. "It's very special to me, and, like my mother, it is irreplaceable."

Simon, the only one with a Fedora, speaks. "Ma'am, I apologize. I found it laying on the floor beside the beds." He explains tritely. The ranch hands have shared living space. Only the Lead hand, Louie, has his own quarters, and I know that he didn't take my beloved mother's brooch. He just returned from family leave this morning.

"Then how did it get there?" I quiz him. But he just shakes his head, looking at the floor.

"I suggest that whoever did it confess. Otherwise, *all* of you are fired." I say firmly. "I cannot have thieves living under my roof."

See how you can tell right away what the genre is? And you're already asking yourself who stole the brooch? And what's going to happen to them?

From 'Proceed with Caution' (Sandra Alex)

"Tube Top Tuesdays!" I bark. "Are you serious?" My face turns as red as a tomato as Mary holds up a hanger, draped with a multitude of different colors of tube tops. Covering my heated cheeks, my expression says I am half aghast, and half *'are we really going to do this?'*. "You've GOT to be kidding! I'm NOT wearing one of those!"

"We're ALL wearing one!" Mary insists, tossing each one on her bed. We both giggle over the AC/DC playing in the background. Her house is empty for the next five minutes, when we expect the other two of our work girlfriends to arrive.

"I wouldn't be caught dead in one."

Mary feigns a glare. "And you're not wearing those glasses, either."

"Really?" I place my hands on my hips. "And how do you suppose I'm going to be able to see? Or shall I just walk into the walls?"

See, again, how you can tell that this is steamy, fun, and you can't wait to read how interesting their night is going to be.

From 'Crossing Boundaries' (Sandra Alex)

It was a struggle. After ten years I finally did it. Not one day passed when I ever considered doing the unthinkable, even though Nick did it all the time without a second thought. As I stand in front of my dresser, clad in layers of clothes I haven't worn since...well, never mind since when. Luckily, they still fit, and so does my wedding ring. Pulling it off my finger, I realize that in nearly ten years of marriage, not once did I take my wedding band off. Underneath it, the skin is flat and shiny, like I've been sitting on my finger for an hour. My whole hand looks odd and feels no better. Nick never wore his wedding ring, or at least, he did when he had to, during family events and pictures and things, but the moment he was home, off it came. He hated wearing it. I hated that he hated wearing it. It's stupid, I know. A lot of things about our marriage were stupid.

This one you can tell is going to be a more angsty romance, more emotional, and that's exactly what I wanted to come across. But you want to read on and see why she's ruminating, right? And why it's taken her so long to take her ring off? And most of all, what's going to happen next?

From 'Dress Rehearsal' (Sandra Alex)

As I watch my road manager's face turn from stone to pasty behind the glass of the telephone booth, I'm trying to imagine what could possibly be worse than this. The tour bus broke down...twice. While they were relatively minor fixes, they still delayed our ETA in San Francisco by two hours. We're opening for a headlining band called 'Snake', who is on a world tour. The bus stinks like sweat, old cigarettes, piss, stale beer, cheap gas, and if you take a cleansing breath, you can smell my bandmate Ivan's puke from earlier. A lovely combination, which is only punctuated by the smell of deep-fried fast food coming from the restaurant parking lot where we're sitting.

So, it's very obvious what's going on here, also, that it's about a rock star. But you want to know if they're going to make it to the concert in time, right?

The idea is to leave more questions than answers. Just like in your blurb (which we'll get to in another book). You have to tell the reader just enough of what's going on, but not too much. And you also need to give a feel or flavor for what the rest of the book has in store. Keep them on their toes!

Writing Style-as Individual as Your Own Reflection

I've read hundreds of books, and I have to say that each of those books reflected a different writing style. Some were better than others, but all were individual in their own way.

During a conversation with a fellow author working on her first novel, it occurred to me that aspiring writers may be struggling with establishing what their writing style is; and more importantly, questioning it and second-guessing it.

When you write something, especially if it's your first time, the most important thing is to get past that first draft. That is often the most difficult task because as a first-time writer, you're always wondering if your manuscript can be better. You find yourself looking at other people's writing style and thinking 'hey, this is great writing; I should do something like this'. Then you wind up deleting more than half of your manuscript and starting from scratch.

What happens then is a destructive pattern of second-guessing, re-writing, editing and back to second-guessing again.

Stephen King, in his book 'On Writing' suggests having a 'closed-door period' where you sit by yourself in whatever area you feel most productive and close the door; allowing nothing or nobody to see your work until the first draft is complete. This also entails you to simply write without looking back. <u>Remember</u>: *the first draft is supposed to be terrible*. **But you can't edit an incomplete book and you can't complete a book if you keep editing it**.

Your writing style will be just that: *your* writing style. The great thing about this is that there is no right or wrong, and the worst thing about this is that there is no right or wrong.

As an aspiring author, you must find your style and be proud of it and comfortable writing it. It has to be a style that **you enjoy reading yourself**. Often, writers find their own style as a hybrid of their favourite author's writing styles...and <u>that's okay</u>.

Even if you write an entire manuscript, let it 'stew' and then read it through and hate it; that's okay too. The important thing is to get it complete; because once you've made your way through an entire manuscript it becomes practice, and the next time it will be easier. <u>And don't forget</u>: **it's always easier to go back and edit a complete manuscript than to re-write and then complete it the first time**.

It's also a great motivating factor to type the words 'The End' and it really helps you to climb back on and begin writing another manuscript while your other one is 'stewing'. It gives you confidence that you *can* do it, a feeling of immense pride, and often when you're near the end of your manuscript, you've acquired another book idea.

So keep writing, don't lose hope even if you think your manuscript is terrible; it's probably not as bad as you think. Remember that *you are your own worst critic*. Just get to 'The End' and celebrate! Your book will only get better from there!

Also, as I'm writing this book, I changed my writing style. After more than nine years writing one style, I read a book, loved the style, changed my own for two new series, and the work just flows out of me. It can take time, but once you find a style that you love, you'll find that your creative energy is jet fueled.

Don't be a 'One Hit Wonder'

"Luck is what you have left after you give 100%"

It's a great inspirational quote, isn't it? It's grounding, realistic and puts whatever you've got going on in your life into perspective.

This quote is something that popped into my mind after reading author Russell Blake's blog post "Being Nora Roberts".

The post talks about how some authors just don't get how much work there is involved in getting 'there'. To that coveted spot in the literary world where people are actually buying your books on their own accord, enjoying them, and telling their friends about them. Wow, old fashioned word-of-mouth advertising, who would have thought?

And the post brought me to a place in my mind where I felt good. After reading the post you might wonder why, because most pragmatic posts about the literary world make you want to pack it up and burn whatever book inventory you have.

But why did it make me feel good? Because I read about authors who simply hope to be overnight successes, who simply decided to become an author on a whim.

And I realized, with great relief, that I'm not one of those authors.

I know there are hundreds more of me out there, who also have been at it for years, and that's great but there are also hundreds if not thousands out there who are just out to make it big on one book.

Don't do that.

Authors, from my heart to yours: if you're a true author who has dreamed of doing this for a long time, then you have dozens of books that are itching to be written, oozing from inside your brain. If your one and only book is already out, don't be a one hit wonder. Write another book.

The reality is it's those authors who have multiple titles available, that are the ones that are going to swim, the others will likely sink.

<u>Ways to avoid being a one hit wonder</u>:
1. Read, read, for God sakes, read!
2. Write every day. It does not matter how much, just keep at it.

If you're truly a writer, then those two things will be laughable to accomplish. Because you're already doing it...and some more, too.

Back to the quote. Most people think that luck is some divine thing that just pops into their life spontaneously, unexpectedly, and without effort. Most foolish people, that is. However, the smarter ones will think about all the things they need to do to get something accomplished, and THEN add a little luck in at the end.

That's the way to do it. Give your 100% into writing books. Plural. Don't sink, don't give up, and don't be a one hit wonder.

Denice Simms

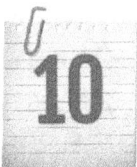

How to Format a Book

in Ten Minutes a Day

My book is born. But it doesn't *look* like a book. I don't know where to start so it appears organized and professionally done.

Is this you?

If you've written a story, whether it be fact or fiction, or you have an idea in mind, and you don't know how to start so it looks as good as bestselling authors' books do, this book is for you.

Having written, formatted, and self-published over thirty novels, I've learned through many years of mistakes, wasted money, and feeling like a failure, how to make a book look just like it came out of a publishing house.

Topics included:

Formatting Your Title Page
ISBN Numbers
How to Trick Word on the Title Page
Show Formatting
Linking
Copyright

References
Dedication Page
Page Breaks
Table of Contents (TOC)
Box Set TOC
Troubleshooting TOC
A Quick Way to Redo Your Entire TOC
Formatting the Body of Your Book
A Little About Kindle Create
Creating Book Files for all Versions of Your Books
Adding Images for Back Matter
Other Things to Place in Your Back Matter
Formatting for Paperback
Adding Page Numbers
Removing Links
TOC-Paperback
Going Thermonuclear
Autovetter Errors
And more...

This book will show you how to prepare your book (both ebook and paperback versions) for uploading to retailer sites, paying particular attention to the scrutiny of Smashwords (I love Smashwords, don't get me wrong!), including everything from the title page to the back matter. Having never used paid formatting services, I've done it all myself since 2010, so I know a thing or two!

'*How to Format a Book in Ten Minutes a Day*' is a step-by-step guide on how to make your work look like a professional formatted it. It's the perfect amount of handholding, but with fast, clear, efficient procedures to get the job done.

There are no gimmicks in here, no fluff, just quick, easy, concise actions a writer can take to get that book looking like a professional did it!

Keep in Touch!

Join my free newsletter and know about new releases.

It's absolutely **FREE**, there are no strings attached, your information is completely confidential, and you can unsubscribe any time.

All you need is an email address.

To join my newsletter, visit my website www.denicesimms.com.

Did you enjoy this book? You can make a big difference.

Do you know what the difference between an author that sells a few copies of their book a month and a New York Times bestselling author is?

The answer is clear and simple: **REVIEWS**

Don't believe me?

Take a look at any NYT bestselling author and a regular author (like me) and see the difference in the number of reviews.

The fact is clear: **reviews lead to sales. Sales lead to bestseller charts.**

One other simple fact is that many advertisers *won't look at a book* unless it has a minimum of 50 book reviews.

That's where you come in. **I need your help**.

Honest reviews of my books help bring them to the attention of other readers.

If you've enjoyed this book, I would be very grateful if you could spend just five minutes leaving a review (it can be as short as a like).

Thanks very much,

Denice

Author's Note

Thanks so much for reading '**How to Write a Book in Ten Minutes a Day**'! I truly hope that you were able to garner some knowledge from it! This book comes from years of making mistakes, wasting money, and feeling like a failure. But as you can see, it takes perseverance and time to get anywhere in the literary world. And you'll get there!

If you've written your book and are ready to move on to uploading and self-publishing, check out my next book. I've done this a time or two!

Happy Reading and Writing!

Denice

PS-if you haven't already subscribed to my newsletter, visit my website at www.denicesimms.com and click 'Subscribe' so you won't miss out on important updates, helpful content and even a deal or two!

www.ingramcontent.com/pod-product-compliance
Lightning Source LLC
Chambersburg PA
CBHW030052230526
45471CB00003B/1063